DOGS IN LOVE

DOGS IN LOVE

EDITED BY
J. C. SUARÈS

TEXT BY
JANA MARTIN

PHOTO RESEARCH BY
KATRINA FRIED

WELCOME

NEW YORK

Published in 1998 by Welcome Enterprises, Inc.
588 Broadway, New York, NY 10012
(212) 343-9430 FAX (212) 343-9434

Distributed in the U.S. by Stewart, Tabori & Chang
a division of U.S. Media Holdings, Inc.
115 West 18th Street, New York, NY 10011

Library of Congress Card Catalog Number: 98-85636
ISBN: 0-941807-22-3

Printed and bound in Italy by Arnoldo Mondadori Editore
10 9 8 7 6 5 4 3 2 1

PAGE 1:

**KARL BADEN
POODLE PAW,
SPRINGFIELD, MASSACHUSETTS, 1992**

"This Standard Poodle had a zirconium brooch clasped
in its ear and a matching diamond on its toenail."

PAGE 2:

**PHILIP GENDREAU
BY THE WATER,
U.S., 1930s**

Best of friends, a tousle-haired girl named Phyllis
and Pal, her equally tousled Wire-haired Fox Terrier,
take a break from playing to rest on a favorite rock.

PAGE 6:

**ROBIN SCHWARTZ
BANDIT AND LONI,
CONNECTICUT, 1997**

"These two Smooth-coated Fox Terriers are
half-sisters from the same breeder, and everything
about them is very sweet. Even their names are sweet.
Bandit, the younger one, bears the full name Rapidan
Heartstrings, and Loni, the dog with the darker mask,
is known as Ch. Heart's Desire. You could say it's
in their blood to be this sweet, since their mother's
name is Ch. Foxmoore Tess Trueheart."

PAGE 7:

**ROBIN SCHWARTZ
CUTTER AND ROCKY,
COLTS NECK, NEW JERSEY, 1994**

"I take my own dogs lure coursing, and these Borzois were
there to race that day too. They were hanging out in the
back of a car, waiting out the rain. They were from the
same litter, which helps explain why they were so
connected. They had the same personality, though I found
out recently that one still races, and the other doesn't."

W

hat are the sure signs that you're in love? Remember that high school crush that took place entirely in the halls, consisting of you passing a certain person, probably named Eric or Stacey, and feeling your heart race and your stomach jump? Suddenly, you lost interest in everything: lunch, math, your friends, sleep. However unrequited, the crush was all-powerful. It seemed stronger than gravity, pulling every cell in your body toward the object of your fevered affection.

I would venture to say that dogs, when they're in love, behave like high school students. Many spirited dogs behave like adolescents anyway, rebelling against authority and bolting their food. Left alone one Saturday night, my dog, an otherwise independent, vigorously healthy German Shepherd-Gray Wolf hybrid, got depressed and ate all the donuts. But another dog was the test case in really proving my theory.

Julie, my neighbor in Tucson, had a dog named Luscius (pronounced "Loo-shuss") that fell badly in love one spring. He was a mutt, some kind of retriever mixed with either Chow, Pit Bull, or maybe Great Dane. He had a thick brindle coat, a head so broad and flat you could rest a cup of coffee on it (but only while he was sleeping), and a long feathery tail that hung straight out behind him like the flag at the end of an oversized load. At two years old he weighed ninety pounds, and my neighbor, strong as she was, knew that at certain times there was nothing she could do to stop him.

Each morning, Julie and I met in the park with our dogs. We bonded on the fact that we both could throw a mean curveball and, despite our boyfriends, fixed our own cars. We were outdoors women in cut-offs and motorcycle boots, unkempt and unafraid. In high school, neither one of us had been the Stacey type.

Of course like most people we projected a certain amount of this sensibility onto our dogs. We thought of Luscius as an overgrown punk rocker with a good heart who, had he grown up in a more conventional home, might have been a football star. And my dog, said shepherd-wolf, was the ideal companion for three-mile runs in the desert. Incidentally, she let Luscius know from the get-go that in case he was interested, he wasn't her type. Good-naturedly, he accepted the role of buddy instead.

One morning there appeared a certain female in our park, a snow-white Standard Poodle, bedecked in a fussy French clip. She stepped delicately through the grass with a woman almost as well-groomed. We instinctively disapproved of this beribboned dog, who seemed the canine equivalent of that high-school cliché: pampered and sugar-sweet, able to slay male hearts with a single appearance in the school hallway. But among us, the one male heart skipped a beat. For the first time all spring, Luscius stood still.

It turned out that her name was Letitia, though her real name was just "too long to even say." She had just moved with her owner into a tidy yellow cottage on the corner of East Second and Valley: as it was explained, she was just getting used to the new neighborhood. Letitia didn't roll, she didn't fetch, she didn't do much of anything. She just paraded. And suddenly, our easy morning routine was turned upside down.

Each morning when she arrived in the park, trotting airily beside her owner, Luscius would drop whatever he'd been doing and stand still, quivering with nerves. Sticks, bones, balls—all were abandoned so he could stand there in shock. You could feel the turmoil coursing through him. He seemed to be saying, "She's here! Oh my gosh! What do I do?" We tried to advise him to stay away. "She's trouble," Julie explained when she tugged him off course from his first attempt at a visit. But a crush is a crush: all sense of rational behavior goes out the window.

On the decisive morning, after a night of heavy rains, Letitia showed up in pink ribbons. She'd just been to her weekly visit at the groomer's, and her coat looked like a cloud. Luscius gallantly rolled in the mud. "Attaboy," Julie said, not realizing he'd done it as a kind of preparation, perhaps trying to conceal his formidable doggy smell. As he keened in Letitia's direction, all senses directed her way, Julie took hold of the leash. "Oh no," she said. "He's buzzing."

The next move was all Luscius. Ears pricked, eyes wide, nose high in the air, tail erect and chest forward, Luscius coiled himself like a spring and then bolted down the green slope towards Letitia. Julie knew better than to hang on. For Luscius, it was a minute's gallop down the hill. Letitia, at the time, was sitting up on her haunches in the sun, waving her pink toenails at her owner. Sensing Luscius, she turned her slender head. Then her owner turned her head as well.

At the sight of this giant furball running for her dog, the owner's face turned a stricken pale, and then for some reason, she picked up Letitia and raced for the useless cover of a tree. My neighbor Julie was chasing Luscius, her henna'd hair flying behind her, yelling, "Hey, stop!" but to no avail. What happened next was the kind of brave maneuver that can make or break an affair: Luscius, having reached his lady love, leaped. He leaped right for Letitia, as if he was going to snatch her in mid-air and fly her off to paradise. But Letitia's owner held the poodle tight. So the leap sent everyone— Letitia, her owner, and Luscius on top—tumbling to the soggy, messy ground.

It was, for all concerned, a moment of terrible failure.

Whether it was the municipal mud soaking into her tennis whites, or the sight of her snowy pride and joy turned entirely a different color, or the way Luscius, exhilarated from his moment of heroism, launched into a song of deafening barks to proclaim that Letitia was his, we'll never know. But in the storm that ensued there were threats of a lawsuit, of calling animal control, and at the very least never seeing us in the park again without calling the police. During all that time, as Julie and I tried to calm down Letitia's owner, Luscius and his poodle were now romping up and down the green hills together, though I noticed that with the skill of a femme fatale, Letitia was always in the lead. As her owner berated us, they were the picture of puppy love. However brief, however disastrous, I think for Luscius it was all worth it.

—Jana Martin

My husband Marc's little dog Suzette got us back together. Marc and I had split up after two years because we thought we wanted different things—a modern story, but dogs aren't modern. I like to think Suzette couldn't stand life without me. She'd run up to women on the street and jump all over them, looking for me. So Marc met a lot of women, but none of them liked him. Then Suzette ran away and wound up at my house, almost a mile away. When Marc came over to take her home, she hid under my bed and refused to come out. Cupid just took over from there.

MADELINE VISALLE, PARIS

RIGHT:
KARL BADEN
DACHSHUND UNDER DRESS,
RHODE ISLAND, 1992

"I couldn't tell whether this Miniature Longhaired Dachshund was scared, or whether it just loved being surrounded by the shelter of its handler's skirt."

MARY ELLEN MARK
SYLVESTER STALLONE AND HIS DOG,
LOS ANGELES, CALIFORNIA, 1991

A portrait of the muscular movie star
and his equally muscular dog.

PAGE 16:

KARL BADEN
MASTIFF AND BOY WITH GLASSES,
MASSACHUSETTS, 1993

"I saw this Mastiff and the little boy at a busy
dog show. They were taking a break from the
goings-on to exchange secrets in private."

PAGE 17:

MARY ELLEN MARK
CAPTAIN MAYA MILLER AND HER DOG,
RENO, NEVADA, 1990

Pro-choice activist and ranch owner Maya Miller,
then seventy-two, with her German Shepherd.

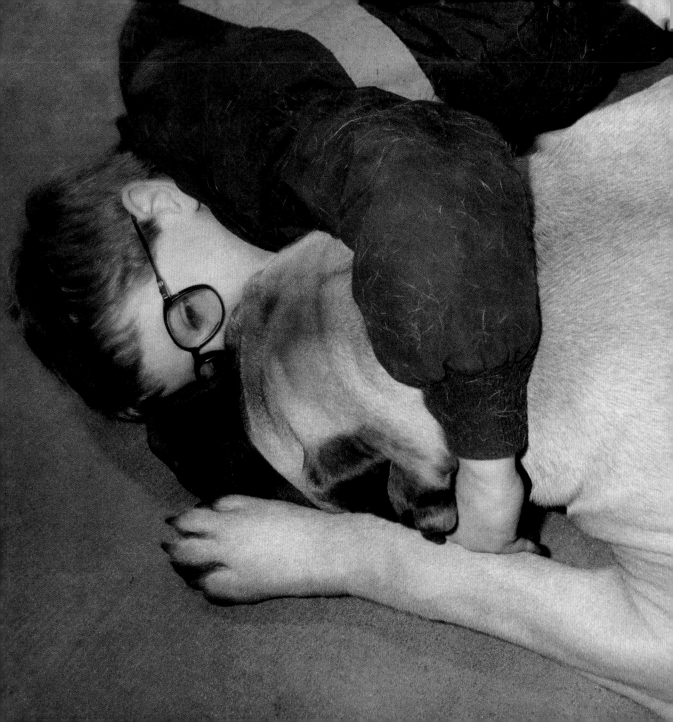

My Black Labrador Retriever, Vanilla, had always regarded me as his number one. But he dumped me for my son Shannon. They fell in love over the course of Shannon's recuperation from breaking a leg while playing softball. The affair began subtly, but I could tell. The signs were: Vanilla lay by Shannon's feet when we watched television instead of by mine. Then Vanilla began to stay in Shannon's room instead of mine. Then, worst of all, he stopped barging in on me when I was in the shower. Instead, he did it to Shannon. That was the last straw. I was heartbroken.

JOHN STOUGHTON, LANDSCAPER, VERMONT

RIGHT:
MARK ELLEN MARK
GAP SHOES, CALIFORNIA, 1992
"This dog is a model. It took time
to teach him to hold the shoe."

OVERLEAF:
UPI PHOTOGRAPHER
FISHING, PONTIAC, MICHIGAN, 1970
Nine-year-old Lewis Flack and his dog, a terrier-hound
mix, spend a quiet afternoon waiting for the fish to bite.

18

There's a really handsome Weimaraner named Chester who comes to work every day with his owner. He's a Wegman dog, very friendly and well-behaved. Instead of cooping him up in the office all day, his owner lets him wander the halls. This means that Chester's free to stand by the front door of the office down the hall and wait for Romeo, another Weimaraner, to come out to play. Romeo, who was rescued from the pound, is a little more hyper, and doesn't come in everyday. When he does, his owner keeps him inside until the end of the day, when most everyone's gone home and Romeo can't get into trouble. But Chester will sit in front of that office door all day, waiting until his pal finally comes out.

ALICE WONG, EDITOR, NEW YORK

RIGHT:
ROLF ADLERCREUTZ
DOG MEETS DOG,
STOCKHOLM, SWEDEN, 1984

"I was taking photographs in this park on a June day, during an art exhibition. The park was filled with sculptures. Along came this dog, and as he passed this sculpture, he turned and looked up at it. Then he went over and sat down, as if he had recognized an old friend and wanted to catch up on old times."

Sheba was a malnourished wreck when I found her under a dumpster. Aside from a broken leg, she had snaggly fangs, stick-out ribs, and enormous ears. Coyote-dog crosses are common in the Southwest, and I figured, either she's wild or not. But I didn't exactly trust her. Naturally my irresponsible neighbors skipped town and left their rabbit behind. I was frantic Sheba would kill it, so I had to take it in. I kept them separated for weeks, though Sheba really wanted to get to this rabbit, and this dumb rabbit seemed to want to get to her. Then the day came when I got home and found the bedroom door open, the rabbit cage open, and the rabbit gone. I was frantic, imagining the worst. But instead I found them nestled together on the couch in the den, which is where they sleep to this day.

TERRY CARERRA, SEDONA, ARIZONA

RIGHT:
**JOHN DRYSDALE
STAND-IN PUP,
NORFOLK, ENGLAND, 1975**

"Having just had her pups sold, the bulldog was feeling rather forlorn, and needed something else to mother. Her owner, a farmer, found an abandoned baby squirrel a few days later and decided to try it with the dog. Acceptance was instant, and the squirrel became an honorary pup."

RIGHT:

UPI PHOTOGRAPHER
WOODSTOCK AND BONITA,
SAN DIEGO, CALIFORNIA, 1975

According to thirteen-year-old Penny Adams, owner
of both Woodstock the mouse and Bonita the Great
Dane, Woodstock walks all over Bonita, and Bonita
doesn't mind a bit. It all started when Woodstock
jumped out of Penny's hand one day and landed on
the dog's head. Bonita, a gentle giant, just stood still.

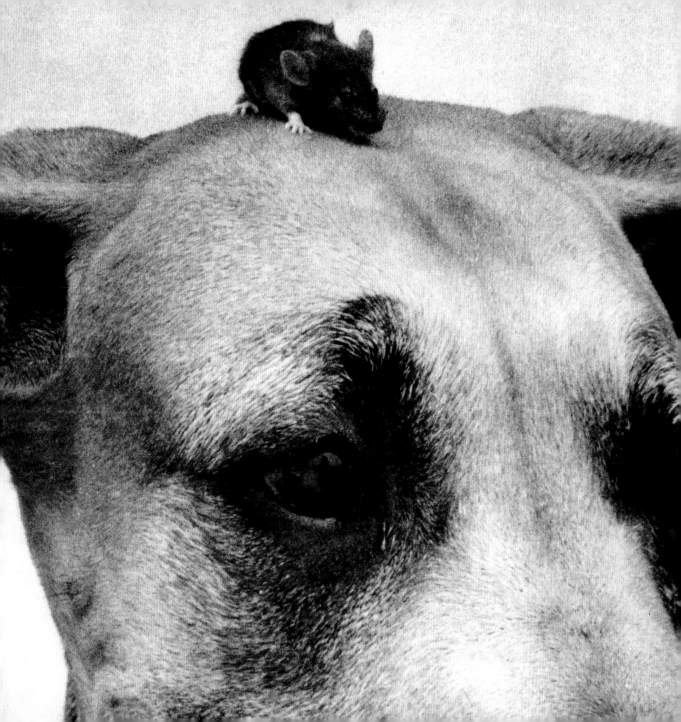

Nowadays you get all this bad press about the Pit Bull. How they eat other dogs and cats and kids and all this. Well, I think maybe it's the owners who put them up to it. Because when I was a kid, I had a dog who looked just like Petey the Pup, and she was the sweetest creature on earth. Her name was Melva, a made-up name, but it sounded right to me. Melva was like a four-legged angel sent down to cheer everyone up. Our cat had kittens, and Melva would lie very still while they crawled all over her. One even fell asleep laying across her paw, so she couldn't get up without disturbing it. For hours, even through dinner time, she wouldn't move. I think she loved the way that kitten felt.

HAROLD SPARKLEY, RETIRED, KANSAS CITY

RIGHT:

UNIDENTIFIED PHOTOGRAPHER
I'LL TAKE CARE OF YOU, U.S., 1940s

A basketful of orphaned kittens arouses the
maternal instinct in a spotted Pit Bull Terrier.

OVERLEAF:

ROBIN SCHWARTZ
NATHANIEL AND REBECCA,
HOBOKEN, NEW JERSEY, 1996

"These are my kids. Nathaniel is a Cornish Rex
cat, and Rebecca's a Whippet and was just
three or four months old when I took this picture.
She loves that cat. She really loves that cat.
My husband thinks they look alike."

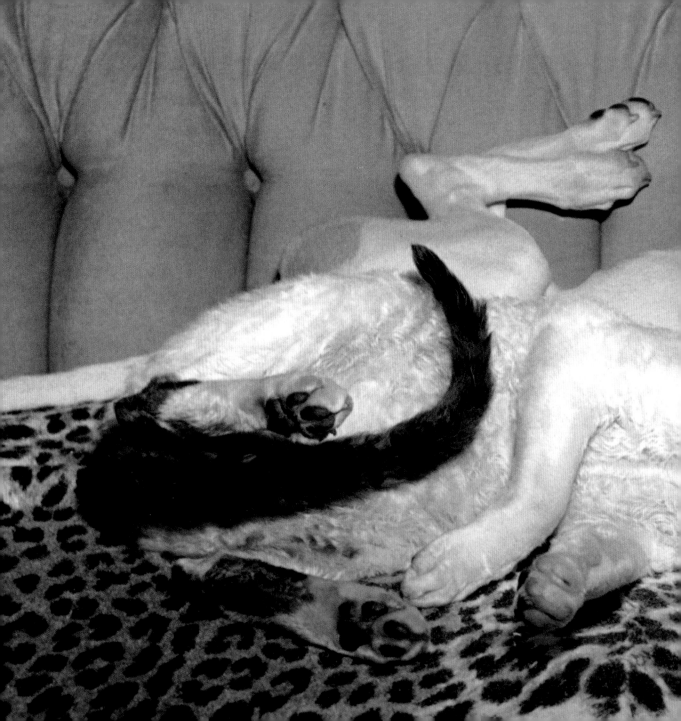

ABOVE:

YLLA
UNTITLED, NEW YORK, 1950

In the photographer's studio, a Wire-haired
Fox Terrier puppy nuzzles a tabby kitten.

RIGHT:

JOHN DRYSDALE
CARPETBAGGERS, ANDOVER, ENGLAND, 1996

"After a lion cub wandered away from its mother at a lion reserve
near Andover, none of the other nursing lionesses would show signs
of maternal possession. Instead, the cub was raised on a bottle in
the secretary's house, in the company of the house's Golden
Retriever. The two spent most of the day on the carpet in the
reception office, forcing visitors to shuffle around them. Of course
no one with even half a heart would have told them to move."

RIGHT:

**UPI PHOTOGRAPHER
PRETTY DOG GOIN' GOOD,
MEMPHIS, TENNESSEE, 1960**

With his hind paws resting on the back of the bicycle
seat and front paws hooked over his owner's
shoulders, Queenie, a Cocker Spaniel–Fox Terrier
mix, takes a ride with fifteen-year-old Mike Miller.

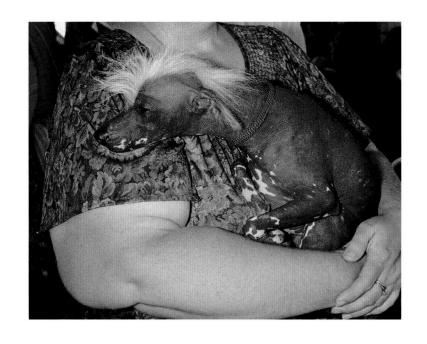

KARL BADEN
CHINESE CRESTED AND BIG WOMAN,
NEW ENGLAND, 1992

"This was at a dog show during a period of time when I'd given myself a hundred-mile radius to work in. Chinese Cresteds are a hairless breed, so they probably like to keep warm. 'Come to Mama,' this dog's handler seemed to be saying."

HARRY HAMBURG
SO LONG OLD BUDDY,
WASHINGTON, D.C., 1998

President Clinton bids adieu to the First Labrador, possibly his
most cherished presidential gift, before taking off for Europe.

When we had our first son, Billy, I was really nervous that my dog Noodle, who is a pretty small dog, would feel threatened by the arrival of this new creature. Noodle was old and pretty set in his ways. Instead, he put me to shame. One day Billy was sick and I didn't even know it. While napping, he must have been crashing around his crib, but there wasn't any noise coming from the baby monitor. Noodle came running in to get me and wouldn't leave me alone until I followed him into Billy's room. Sure enough, Billy had a high fever. From then on, Noodle was the self-appointed nanny.

CARLA DROSNICK, MOTHER, IOWA CITY

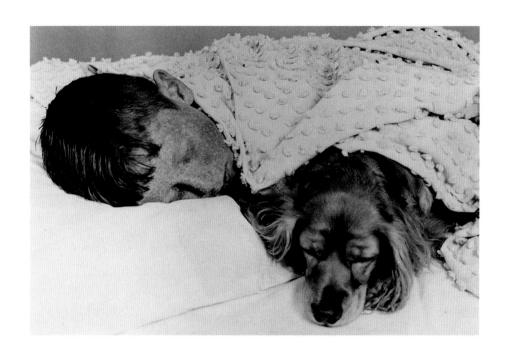

**UNIDENTIFIED PHOTOGRAPHER
NAPTIME,
U.S., 1950s**

A young boy's sleep is made sweeter by the
presence of his Cocker Spaniel sharing the blanket.

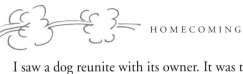

I saw a dog reunite with its owner. It was the best demonstration of joy I've ever seen. I'd found the dog, a retriever cross, wandering around lost on a Friday night. I didn't find its owner until Monday. The dog spent the weekend curled up in a miserable ball in my shop as I worked. Friends came in and out; it didn't stir. I brought it food; it didn't eat a thing. Monday morning, it suddenly began crying like a puppy and scratching at the front door. It must have sensed the owner coming. When she walked in the door, the dog leaped straight into her arms, yowling hysterically. It seemed to be saying, "My love, my love, I'll never leave you again."

KURI SAWAI, SURFBOARD DESIGNER, HILO, HAWAII

RIGHT:

UNIDENTIFIED PHOTOGRAPHER
A DOG AND HIS BOY, U.S., 1930s

Silhouetted against an afternoon sky, boy and dog—
a young shepherd-retriever mix—stand face to face.

DONNA RUSKIN
DIAMOND JIM,
NEW YORK CITY, 1988

"In Central Park I came across this man and his dog, a Standard Poodle
named Diamond Jim. The man was clearly very proud of the dog. I got
the sense that the two of them had rehearsed this kissing stunt before.
Perhaps they were trying to show each other off to their best advantage."

RIGHT:

INTERNATIONAL NEWS PHOTOGRAPHER
PRODIGALS FROM PRAGUE,
NEW YORK, 1940

Mrs. Andrew Gilchrist, the wife of the then-U.S. Vice Consul at Prague,
with her Great Dane Gollo, returning to the states on the U.S.S. *Manhattan*.

CHARLES G. SNYDER
IN THE HOLIDAY SPIRIT,
BOSTON, MASSACHUSETTS, 1946

Brimming over with Christmas spirit, Lee the cat forgets his innate antipathy
for anything canine long enough to give Frisco the Chihuahua a huge hug.

RIGHT:

ABBY HODES
UNTITLED, NEW YORK, 1997

"At a sidewalk cafe one spring night, everything felt very French:
the conversation, the menu, even the dogs. One of them had been
standing around like it owned the place. When the other dog came up, the
two greeted each other like Parisians, kissing each other on both cheeks."

"Kiran is a white German Shepherd who weighs about
a hundred pounds, and Foster's a female Pug. They live
downstairs from me — Kiran in the apartment above
Foster—and they're about the same age. A lot of dogs
are afraid of Kiran, but not Foster. They really like
each other, and play together as much as they can."

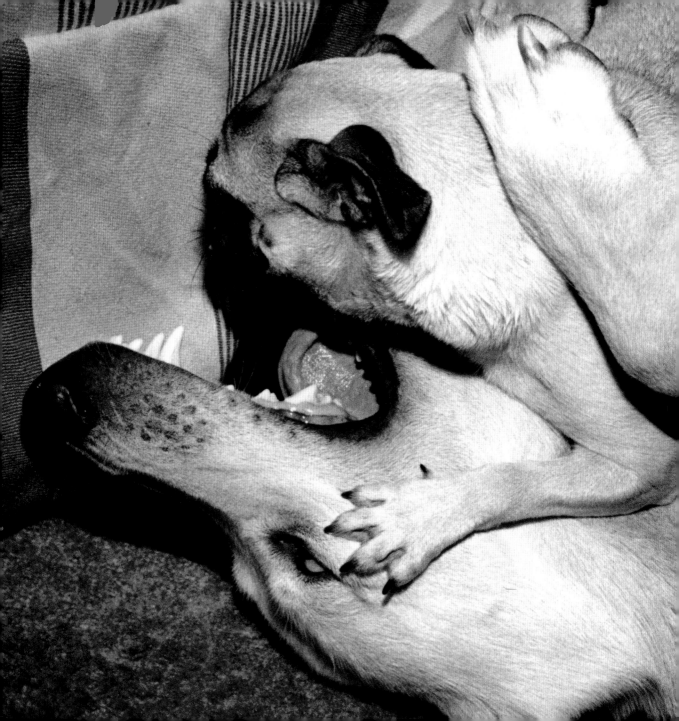

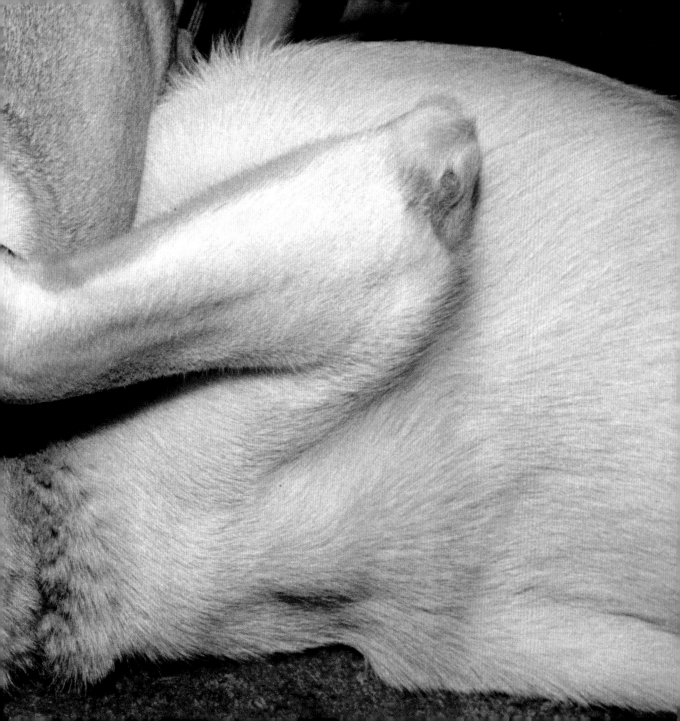

PREVIOUS PAGES:

ROBIN SCHWARTZ
CAZI AND SATIN,
RUTHERFORD, NEW JERSEY, 1998

"These are two Bedlington Terriers at nine-thirty in the morning, when they're usually not awake. Their owners work all week, and this was Saturday. But the dogs don't understand the difference between a Saturday morning and a workday morning, so as I was photographing them, they just fell asleep. Satin, the youngest of these two girls, is quite attached to Cazi (short for Cashmere), and really looks up to the other older dog. She follows Cazi everywhere, watching and mimicking. Younger dogs just want to be in the older dog's world."

RIGHT:

ROBIN SCHWARTZ
ALPHI AND MISTY DAVENPORT,
FEASTERVILLE, PENNSYLVANIA, 1996

"These two Salukis are from the same breeder, and are both very sweet dogs. Alphi, the white one, is a one-year-old male, and Misty, the cream one, is four. Here they'd just been playing like crazy and were completely exhausted."

I taught my dog Geraldo (a Bouvier) to hold a flower in his

mouth and bring it to my wife, in an effort to show my wife that

I actually do have the capacity for silly little romantic gestures.

But the result is that my wife gives the dog all the credit.

BOB ROSS, TEACHER, MIAMI

RIGHT:
KARL BADEN
PUG WITH GOWN AND FEET,
WORCESTER, MASSACHUSETTS, 1993
"For Halloween the Pug wore butterfly wings, and the
girl wore a diaphanous robe with angel's wings to match."

Jess, a mutt, stands under the high-slung chassis of her Great Dane pal Ramah. According to owner Mrs. Olive Tate of Upton Road, if you combine one's size and the other's barking, you've got a terrific watchdog.

RIGHT:

**ACME PHOTOGRAPHER
THE LONG AND THE SHORT OF IT,
CHELSEA, ENGLAND, 1947**

During the Allied Forces Memorial Fund Show at the People's Dispensary for Sick Animals in Chelsea, a giant St. Bernard named She stands protectively over her best friend, a Miniature Dachshund named Mitzi.

RIGHT:

**ROBIN SCHWARTZ
WEDDING,
CONNECTICUT, 1996**

"This dog, a Boxer, was the bride's dog. Not only was he
present at the wedding, he was extremely excited about
it. The whole affair was held in a glass church built like
a triangle. On a nice sunny day it's probably beautiful,
but as it happened, the wedding took place during a
nor'easter, which really added to the drama of the
occasion. But the Boxer wasn't scared. He just got more
and more excited the nastier it got outside. And he loved
being in the middle, between the bride and groom."

OVERLEAF:

**KARL BADEN
HARLEQUIN DANES,
MASSACHUSETTS, 1993**

"At a Great Dane match I came across a woman in a
harlequin T-shirt, getting love from her giant."

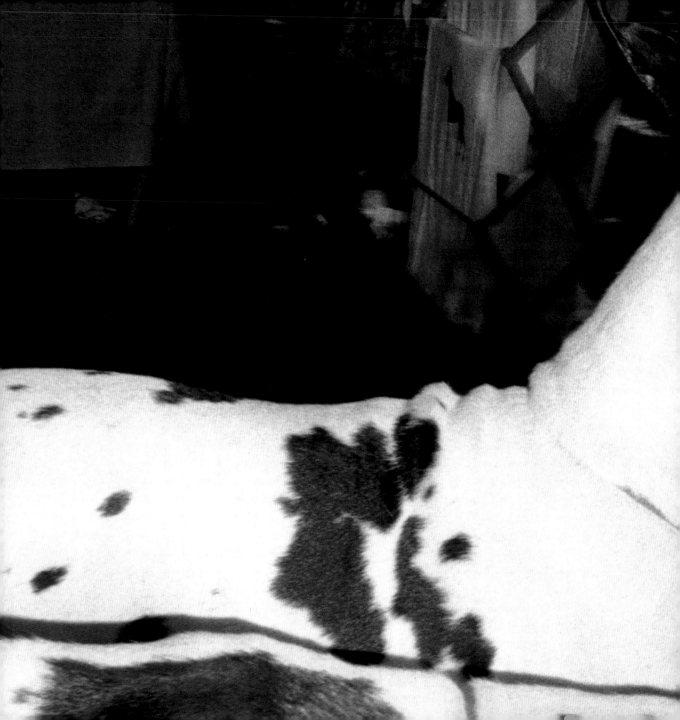

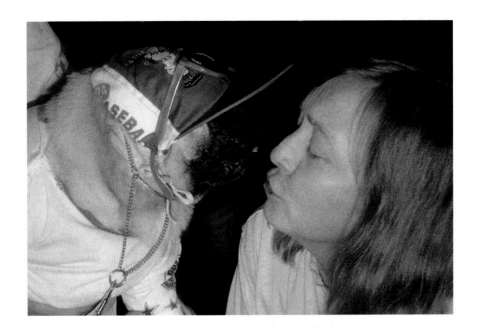

KARL BADEN
RED SOX PUG,
MASSACHUSETTS, 1993

"At a Pug Easter Parade, this entry wore a
uniform that was practically regulation,
ready to slug one out of the park for its owner."

RIGHT:

KARL BADEN
CHARLOTTE LICKING GIRL,
CAMBRIDGE, MASSACHUSETTS, 1991

"My wife's late dog Charlotte, a shepherd mutt, was a great
dog who loved everybody. The little girl on our sofa was from
down the block, and liked Charlotte especially. In fact she
came over specifically to visit with Charlotte, not with us."

Caramel, my Viszla male, got into the habit of jumping onto the couch and pressing his nose against the window every day at three o'clock. He'd give a little yap, then race around to the front door.

Then he'd sit there gallantly, waiting for me to open it. When I did, he'd walk, with all the dignity he could muster, up to the edge of the driveway, and sit there like a statue. A minute later the love of his life, a female Viszla, would come trotting up with her owner. I knew Caramel wanted to bust out with joy, but he didn't. He 'd wait for her to come up, and then they'd politely touch noses. As she'd prance away, he'd turn around and maintain his composure until he got back inside. Then he'd fall into crazy spasms of joy and knock over the furniture.

LILA CARROLL, ILLUSTRATOR, CHICAGO

RIGHT:
DONNA RUSKIN
TOMBSTONE TILLIE AND CALAMITY JANE,
PENLAND, NORTH CAROLINA, 1992

"These two characters, mutts with a lot of Labrador Retriever in them, are lounging in the side yard of Suzanne Ford's bed-and-breakfast in Penland. Suzanne told me that they were strays and had just showed up one day. Being the hospitable type, she took them in, and they never left."

**JOHN DRYSDALE
ODD FRIENDS,
ANDOVER, ENGLAND, 1991**

"The puma cub, starring in a movie, was given the company of a friendly English Pointer when it wasn't on the set. The two became so close that the dog adopted the puma and moved it into the house."

OVERLEAF:

**H.D. BARLOW
UNCONDITIONAL LOVE,
U.S., 1940s**

No matter what Freddie does, Karl the Dachshund is always there. And if Freddie begins to cry, Karl responds with an almost motherly show of concern, putting a reassuring paw on the baby's arm and licking his tears away.

RIGHT:

**JOHN DRYSDALE
BACK TO BACK,
YORKSHIRE, ENGLAND, 1968**

"The llama was bought for a children's play area at a hotel
but was too shy for the other llamas there, who picked on
it. Instead this social reject turned to a resident
Rhodesian Ridgeback for consolation. The two became
not only fast friends, but the children's favorites too.
Everyone wanted to see the llama and the big dog."

OVERLEAF:

**ROBIN SCHWARTZ
ISIS AND TINA,
PISCATAWAY, NEW JERSEY, 1996**

"The big white Borzoi is four months old here, and
Tina, the Whippet, is three months old. They share
the same last name of McDonald, and they're cousins.
You can tell right off that they like each other.
Sighthounds sleep a lot, and these two love to sleep arm
in arm. At this age, Tina was like Isis' baby.
Even for a Borzoi, Isis was very tall."

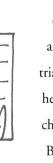

Buffy, my dog, was with me for eighteen years. She was your basic medium brown mutt, looked a little like a Basenji with her pointy ears, and weighed no more than forty pounds. But she was an amazing dog. Once she even got me out of a legal jam. I was on trial on campus in Buffalo, falsely charged with the stabbing of the head of campus security. Those were, after all, radical times. For a character reference, my physics professor wrote a letter about how Buffy was always a fixture on campus, following me everywhere, and how someone with such a great dog couldn't possibly be an evil or violent person. As this letter was being read in the courtroom, my friends stood outside the doors with my dog. When the reader got to the part about Buffy, they opened the doors and let Buffy in. She came trotting through the courtroom right up to me, and curled up at my feet. It was a very Norman Rockwell moment, and all the proof they needed to drop the charges.

ELIOT SHARP, COMPOSER, NEW YORK CITY

RIGHT:
UNIDENTIFIED PHOTOGRAPHER
MON AMI, PARIS, 1960s
In a café at the Beat Hotel, a ever-watchful terrier-mix named Biquette assumes his customary place atop the shoulders of owner Madame Madeleine, a concierge from Place St. Michel.

JOHN DRYSDALE
MONKEY MOTHER CARE,
BANBURY, ENGLAND, 1990

"This young chimpanzee was being reared in-house.
The owner also bred Jack Russell Terriers. When the
chimp was shown a puppy, it was fascinated and tried
to mother it. The puppy welcomed the attention."

OVERLEAF:

TEDDY AARNI
COLLIES, STOCKHOLM, 1980s

Is it just breed recognition, or something stronger?
Two rough-coated Collies touch noses in
profile, creating a regal silhouette.

Text: Jana Martin
Drawings: J.C. Suarès
Photo Research: Katrina Fried
Design: Tania Garcia